FAITH
AND SCIENCE
IN THE 21ST CENTURY

*A POSTMODERN PRIMER FOR
YOUTH AND ADULTS*

8-Session Guide
Downloadable Video and Audio Resources Available Online

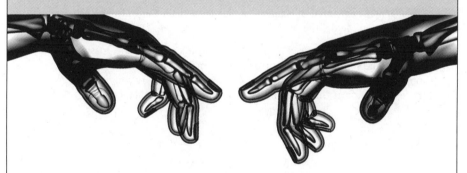

Peter M. Wallace, Editor
Henry L. Carrigan Jr., Writer

=== FEATURING: ===

*Scott Hoezee • Ted Peters • Katharine Jefferts Schori • Nicholas Knisely
David Wood • Nancy Duff • Tom Long • Luke Powery*

CHURCH
PUBLISHING
INCORPORATED

Day1®

The Day1 Faith & Science in the 21st Century project was made possible through the support of a grant from the John Templeton Foundation. The opinions expressed in this project are those of the authors and do not necessarily reflect the views of the John Templeton Foundation.

Church Publishing
19 East 34th Street
New York, NY 10016
www.churchpublishing.org

Cover design by Marc Whitaker, MTWdesign
Typeset by Denise Hoff

For Day 1 Faith and Science Series:
Peter M. Wallace, Executive Producer and Host
Donal Jones, Director of Production

Library of Congress Cataloging-in-Publication Data

A record of this book is available from the Library of Congress.

ISBN-13: 978-1-64065-047-3 (pbk.)
ISBN-13: 978-1-64065-048-0 (ebook)

Printed in the United States of America

"When we look at the world God made and learn more about it through science and discovery, we connect this to the death and resurrection of the Jesus, who also created it all and who has redeemed it all. And then we too can say, 'It's all right. The whole thing, *ta panta*, it's all right.'"

—The Rev. Scott Hoezee

"Instead of lying on the beach sand looking at the sky, we today look through telescopes and monitors and computer graphs. Yet, what we see is just as marvelous and awesome as what our ancestors saw. The universe is as intricate as it is massive, as mysterious as it is understandable, as wondrous as it is glorious. . . . But the Psalmist made another point that remains true today, namely, regardless of how large our cosmos might be, God still loves you and me individually and intimately."

—The Rev. Dr. Ted Peters

"The great arc of the biblical narrative sheds light on how human beings can build healthier and holier relationships with all that is, and with the source of all that is. There are plenty of stories about what goes wrong. . . . Yet the thrust of each part of the narrative leads us back toward our home in the One who has made all that is, and loves it all. We know that reality as God, whom we call love."

—The Rt. Rev. Dr. Katharine Jefferts Schori

"Jesus's words about time and eternity, God's beautiful poetic response to Job, are exactly what we ultimately hope for in our longing to make sense of the senseless. There are no easy answers to the paradox of time and eternity. But God inhabits Eternity and Jesus inhabits Time, and we believe by faith that God is good."

—The Rt. Rev. Nicholas Knisely

"Our work, the work God has given us to do, is to cultivate communities and societies in which the fact of the divine image-bearing nature of humanity becomes self-evident in our regard for one another and for God's good creation."

—The Rev. David Wood

"Only with a sense of gratitude for the animals that God created to populate the world along with us, and only by acknowledging the limits God has placed on our power and freedom to use animals for our benefit, can we take responsibility for their welfare in a manner consistent with being creatures of God ourselves."

—The Rev. Dr. Nancy J. Duff

"The psalmist reminds us that when we look at life through the eyes of faith, the goal is not simply the quantity of life, but the quality of life—the depth and breadth and height of life, not just its length. What makes life good is not just longevity, not just living more and more days, but becoming a certain kind of person, a person whose heart is wise before God."

—The Rev. Dr. Thomas G. Long

"Life has an inexhaustible curriculum, and the lessons are infinite just like God even when it comes to a conversation about faith and science, God and the cosmos, creation and evolution, quantum physics and eternity, *imago dei* and science, genetics and morality, and health and healing. We have so much more to learn."

—The Rev. Dr. Luke Powery

Contents

How to Use This Resource

Who can use this book?

This book will guide your group—whether it's a youth or adult formation class, Bible study group, or other small group—through each session of the Day1 Faith and Science series. Here you'll find all the information to confidently prepare for and guide each session. All group members and any others interested in this important subject are encouraged to purchase a copy of this book to read, study, and explore the online resources personally.

How many sessions are there?

There are eight sessions, each with corresponding resources from one of eight noted Church leaders well versed in theology and science. The first session provides an introduction to the course and the final session explores ways to continue the discussion. The course can be expanded to sixteen sessions if that better fits your needs, with each offering optional discussions and activities.

How do we access the video and audio files?

This course utilizes video and audio content downloadable for a modest charge. The videos and audio files are intended to be played during the sessions. The audio files for each session include a sermon presented by one of the eight speakers along with opening and closing interviews; they originally aired on the national Day1 radio program and podcast (Day1.org).

To access these media files, go online to:

http://day1.org/faithandscience

and follow the instructions for making payment and accessing the files. You can download the files to a laptop and use a media player during the session. Individuals can also download these files to replay them on their own time.

What equipment and supplies are needed for the sessions?

You will need a laptop and Internet connection (Wi-Fi or cable) to access the video and audio files (we suggest you download them prior to the sessions). With a small group, a laptop screen may be sufficient to view the video, but with more than six we suggest you connect the laptop to a large-screen television or to a projector with a screen or blank wall. Be sure to practice the setup and use of the media files beforehand so you won't waste class time figuring it out. A whiteboard or large newsprint pad and markers will enable you to capture observations, questions, and ideas. Pens and paper should be made available to participants for note taking. Have enough Bibles for all participants; different translations would be helpful.

How should we facilitate the sessions?

- You may have one leader for all eight or sixteen sessions, or rotate leaders. Be clear well ahead of time about who will lead each session.

- Someone will need to be responsible for arranging for meeting space, setting up the room for group comfort, and making sure the necessary equipment is there.

- The session leader or other designated person should keep track of time. The leader should engage the group so that all feel free to participate as they wish and keep the conversation moving forward to ensure the topic is covered.

- Be sure to arrange to promote the study with dates, time, and location through appropriate website, email, and social media avenues.

What should we consider about the meeting space?

- In addition to ensuring that your desired space and equipment are available, take some time to make the space inviting and hospitable. You may want to offer coffee, tea, or other beverages and snacks before or during the gathering time.

- Make sure the lights and windows can be dimmed sufficiently to view the video presentation.

- Ensure you have a way of recording your members' comments or points either on an erasable board or a large pad of paper.

- Brainstorm with your group other ways to make the meeting space efficient and welcoming.

How flexible are the sessions time-wise?

This resource is designed to be tailored to your group's needs. Each session can be adjusted from 30 or 45 minutes to an hour or more depending on your own opening and closing activities and the extent of your discussions. Approximate times are given for each portion of every session. The core activities and discussions for each session will run approximately 60 minutes. If your group is large (over twelve), consider breaking into small groups more often than indicated for discussion so everyone will have an opportunity to share. While some of the segments in each session are marked as optional, you may find your time frame requires that you skip other sections as well. You may choose to spend two meetings per session. For evening or weekday groups, you can extend the sessions by using the complete leader's guide, listening together to all audio files featuring the preacher's interviews and message, and giving time for deeper reflection and discussion.

What kinds of interaction are offered?

Throughout each session designated activities are offered with approximate time frames for READing Scripture together, REFLECTing individually, WATCHing video clips, DISCUSSing a given topic, LISTENing to audio clips, and breaking out into pairs, triads, or small groups to **THINK AND SHARE** more intimately. **OPTIONAL ACTIVITIES** may lend themselves to more creative experiences such as drawing, writing, and composing hymns or prayers.

How do we close each session and go from there?

Each session provides closing activities, some "homework" to do before the next session, and a suggested prayer, which you can adapt to reflect your own traditions and wishes. The leader can preview the next session's topic. It's helpful for the group to self-evaluate, either at the end of the session or on their own time, by asking questions such as: What new insights have I experienced in this session? What expanded my learning or changed my thinking in any way? How did the discussion help me understand my relationship with God more fully? What one thing would I like to share with someone else?

Can Science and Faith Inform Each Other?

Does the universe make any sense? Does the cosmos have purpose? And what about us human beings? Do we matter? Is there any way to know? Listen to some people these days, including some vocal scientists, and you will hear the answer loud and clear: "No, not really. We don't matter. We're too small. The universe is pretty much pointless."

—The Rev. Scott Hoezee

■ Background

The quarrel between religion and science has ancient roots. The first philosophers in Greece—such as Heraclitus and Parmenides—actively pursued what we would call scientific questions, thereby challenging the roles of the gods in their culture. They asked questions about the character of human nature, the role of nature in shaping human life, the beginning of human life, and the shape of life after death. Their answers to such questions didn't involve the presence of supernatural forces; they focused instead on the natural world to provide explanations for the way humans interact with each other and the world.

By the end of the nineteenth century, the ongoing conversation between religion and science took on new dimensions with Charles Darwin's writings about evolution. When many people of faith read his books—or heard about them from their pastors—they rejected the idea that human life developed randomly without the involvement of a divine Creator providing and sustaining human life. As the twentieth century brought new scientific advances, such as quantum physics and developments in medicine that could prolong life and intervene in the process of death, even more questions arose for people of faith.

The major questions with which people of faith often grapple—and that are raised by the various speakers in this Day1 Faith and Science series—involve the compatibility of faith and science. For example, can we reconcile creation and evolution? How do new medical technologies alter our understandings of life and death? What about the purpose of life? Do scientists and people of faith have anything meaningful to say to each other?

In this first session, Scott Hoezee, author of *Proclaim the Wonder: Engaging Science on Sunday*, encourages us to think about these questions, focusing on Paul's approach to nature and God in Colossians.

■ Before the Session

Participants may like to come to the session having reflected on the issues to be discussed. The following questions invite participants to engage rationally and spiritually with the topic, so share them in advance announcements of the group study. Encourage participants to jot down notes, questions, and reflections.

1. How does God reveal Godself to you through nature? Through the Bible? Through Jesus? Through the teachings of the Church? Through some other means?

2. What does God reveal to you through nature? Can you have faith in a God who is solely revealed through nature?

3. Is it possible for science and faith to be compatible? If so, how? If not, why not?

4. What views do the biblical writers—the psalmists or Paul, for example—have of the natural world and our place in it?

■ The Group Meeting

WELCOME those attending and if necessary have everyone introduce themselves briefly. Explain the purpose of this series. Open with prayer if you choose.

READ   Colossians 1:15–23   *(2 minutes)*

Have a volunteer read it, read it together, or play Audio File 1-4 to hear Scott Hoezee read it. If possible, read the passage in different translations.

> He is the image of the invisible God, the firstborn of all creation; for in him all things in heaven and on earth were created, things visible and invisible, whether thrones or dominions or rulers or powers— all things have been created through him and for him. He himself is before all things, and in him all

things hold together. He is the head of the body, the church; he is the beginning, the firstborn from the dead, so that he might come to have first place in everything. For in him all the fullness of God was pleased to dwell, and through him God was pleased to reconcile to himself all things, whether on earth or in heaven, by making peace through the blood of his cross.

And you who were once estranged and hostile in mind, doing evil deeds, he has now reconciled in his fleshly body through death, so as to present you holy and blameless and irreproachable before him—provided that you continue securely established and steadfast in the faith, without shifting from the hope promised by the gospel that you heard, which has been proclaimed to every creature under heaven. I, Paul, became a servant of this gospel.

WATCH   Video 1   *(4 minutes)*

REFLECT   *(10 minutes)*

Ponder the passage and Hoezee's comments by considering together some or all of these questions:

- Is this a biblical text that comes to mind immediately when you think about the relationship between faith and science?

- What messages in the passage do you hear about the relationship between faith and science?

- What is Paul's attitude toward creation and all things created?

- What is the purpose of the cosmos?

- What role do creatures play in creation?

- What can we know about God from this passage?

- How can we relate to God and to a scientific view of the world after reading this passage?

- What are Paul's final words in the passage, and how do they relate to the questions about faith and science?

LISTEN Audio File 1-1 *(5 minutes)*

In his opening interview with Day1 host Peter Wallace, Scott Hoezee shares some of his goals in teaching his class on faith and science. He tries to introduce students to the current state of science and to areas of science with which they might be unfamiliar.

DISCUSS *(5 minutes)*

Talk about some of the newest developments in science with which you are familiar. What are some ways that you think religion and science can inform each other in light of new developments in science?

Optional Discussion

Hoezee also talks about revelation and our response to it in this interview:

> Particularly in my Reformed tradition, we've long had this theology of revelation of two books. There's the book of nature, the creation of God, and of course scripture; and of course we believe that due to our sinfulness we can't read the book of nature correctly without—as John Calvin said—putting on the spectacles or the eyeglasses of scripture. But we're always interpreting both books and we can make mistakes on both sides. . . . But there are sometimes conflicts, apparent conflicts, and

the question becomes, where does the mistake lie? Is it in the interpretation of what we're seeing through science, or is the mistake what we thought the Bible was saying all along? . . . We're never going to achieve perfect harmony and shouldn't expect to, I suppose, but come as close as we can to getting both right and then seeing where are the convergences and where are the questions we still have to work out.

Take a few minutes to consider these questions:

- Do we in the church have views of science that are outdated or that need updating?

- Do we have views of the Bible that might be left over from earlier in our lives and that need reconsideration?

- What does reconsideration of our views about science and about the Bible reveal about the relationship of the two?

LISTEN   Audio File 1-2   *(13 minutes)*

In his sermon, entitled "Every Creature," Hoezee raises several questions that relate to science and religion. In one section he discusses purpose and meaning—of human life and of the universe—and he probes the ways that we as people of faith might feel after scientific discoveries that question our role in the universe.

THINK AND SHARE   *(10 minutes)*

Divide into small groups of two or three. Discuss the following questions based on what Hoezee said:

Oh, once upon a time before we knew anything much about how big the universe is, how many billions of stars there are, how many billions of whole galaxies there are—once upon a time we human beings fancied that we mattered, that we were the center of the universe, that the whole thing was finally about little old us. But only the religiously deluded still think that. We now know we are tiny specks of life living on a tiny dust mote of a planet orbiting a tiny pin prick of light we call the sun, but that is just one star among a billion in the Milky Way galaxy alone. So, no, we don't matter. But is that so? Does the universe that science is uncovering in ever-more wondrous detail have no purpose and no meaningful place for humans? And does the Bible that in ever more wondrous detail reveals God have any way to speak into what science reveals?

- How does scientific evidence that the universe is self-regulated, in no need of my existence, make me feel?

- Is there any purpose and meaning in the universe?

- What role does God play in fashioning that meaning and purpose?

- Are there any contemporary scientific views of the universe or of humanity that give meaning and purpose to life and to the world?

- Is the biblical view of the universe and of human life any different from the scientific view of them? If so, in what ways are these two views different?

LISTEN   Audio File 1-3   *(4 minutes)*

Continue with Peter Wallace's follow-up interview with Hoezee.

DISCUSS   *(5 minutes)*

Consider the role of worship in your church:

- How does it proclaim the glory of all creation?

- Do we proclaim the glory and wonder of creation in sermon and song?

- Do we include thanks for our bodies, our health— and our sickness—in our prayers?

- How do our prayers proclaim and embrace the glory of creation?

Optional Discussion

Hoezee makes an important point about worship and glory in his follow-up interview:

> What kind of things do you want to think about when you're also in worship? John Calvin actually has a part in his *Institutes* where he suggests that it's absolutely right in worship to give thanks to God for well-functioning kidneys and spleens, and the . . . physical things we don't often associate with our worship. And again, it's just the idea of seeing that bigger picture and incorporating it into your prayer life, incorporating into worship, into what we think about when we sing, into what we hear in sermons. That's the challenge for preachers. Once that again becomes a habit of mind, it becomes a very natural part of how you frame up your faith all the time.

Optional *Think and Share*

Use one or all of these discussion starters in small groups as time allows:

- How would your church's worship need to change in order to proclaim the glory of God in all creation? How would your own prayer life need to grow in order to proclaim the glory of God in all creation?

- Can we say that we have more reasons to praise God the more we learn about creation through science? Give some examples.

- In what circumstances do we wrestle with questions of meaninglessness?

- Describe science's ability to address such questions, and about religion's ability to address the same questions. For example, when a loved one dies, how can science help us understand and deal with that loss? How can religion help us? Can they complement each other in such a situation?

- How is Jesus a model for embracing the bigness of the universe and the glory of creation? Find a few Bible passages that reflect Jesus's view of the universe as a place that has a purpose, for God or for humanity.

CLOSING CONVERSATION *(5 minutes)*

1. Have each person in the group describe one way that science and faith are compatible.

2. Have each person in the group describe how he or she will try to locate ways that the universe described by science can provide meaning and purpose for humanity.

3. Discuss a way this session has given you a new understanding or expanded view of God's purpose.

FOR NEXT SESSION *(1 minute)*

The next meeting will focus on the topic of God and the cosmos.

- Think about how Hoezee's reflections on meaning and purpose in the universe and in human life lay helpful groundwork for a discussion of God and the cosmos.

PRAYER *(1 minute)*

Dear God of such splendid created wonders, we give you thanks and praise for the gift of the creation and for the further gift we get through Jesus, who has restored that creation and will preserve it for all eternity. We give you thanks for all the opportunities we have even now to see hints and whispers of the world that is to come. And we are so very grateful, O God, for your gift of life, for your love and care for every creature, for all things. We give you thanks and praise, through Jesus Christ our Creator and Redeemer. *Amen.*

God and Cosmos

As we look out into the universe and identify the many accidents of physics and astronomy that have worked together to our benefit, it almost seems as if the universe must in some sense have known we were coming.

—The Rev. Dr. Ted Peters

■ Background

This session focuses on the relationship between God and the world. We don't often use the word *cosmos* today, but people in the ancient world used the word regularly to refer to the order of the universe.

In biblical texts, *cosmos* is opposed to chaos. In the creation story in Genesis 1:1–5, God is depicted as a Creator who brings order out of the chaos of the watery void. The opening verses of this story are so familiar to us that we often don't notice the magnificent orderliness of the creation. In this short passage alone, God not only forms the heavens and the

15

earth but also rhythmically creates an orderly structure—night and day, light and darkness—that provides order to time.

The writers wrote the story against the backdrop of tremendous upheaval in Israel and Judah; the Israelites had lost their land as they were sent into exile in Babylon and their temple—the place around which the nation's life was ordered—had been destroyed. The loss of order was so great that the writer of Psalm 137, who also likely had a hand in the editing and writing of Genesis 1, asks how the exiled people can sing the Lord's song in a strange land. Genesis 1 powerfully reminds the exiled people that God the Creator remains in control of the cosmos and creates order out of what seems like chaos.

In John 3:16, John uses the word *cosmos* to describe the universe. God loves the cosmos (world) so much that God yearns to redeem it by bringing a new order into it in Jesus. Notice that in this Gospel, God is still the Creator who has a particular relationship to the cosmos: God in Jesus sustains the cosmos. In the Greek world in which John was writing, the cosmos referred not only to the world of humanity but also to the entire created order—animals, stars, the heavens. The passage in the gospel of John illustrates the depth and breadth of God's involvement in the cosmos, and it encourages us to reflect on God's relationship to the cosmos and the cosmos' relationship to God.

By the Middle Ages, theologians attempted to prove the existence of God through reason and by using philosophical arguments for God's existence. The argument states that the existence of the cosmos offers the strongest evidence for the existence of God who created it. The cosmological argument asks us to think about ways that we see God in the cosmos and the cosmos in God.

In this session, Ted Peters, who is research professor emeritus in systematic theology and ethics at Pacific

Lutheran Theological Seminary and the Graduate Theological Union in Berkeley, California, and the author of several books on theology and science (including *God— the World's Future: Systematic Theology for a Postmodern Era*), asks us to consider our understanding of God and the cosmos and to think about the differences and similarities in the ways that faith and science describe this relationship.

■ Before the Session

As the group prepares for the second session of the Day1 Faith and Science series, review questions raised in the last session. Think about the challenges you have reflecting on the conversation between faith and science. In what ways is such a conversation meaningful for you? In what ways is the conversation difficult? Reflect on the following questions as you prepare for this week's session.

1. Where have you witnessed the glory of creation this week?

2. How have you incorporated praise for the glory and beauty of creation and all creatures in your prayer and worship life?

3. What biblical passages have you read this week that encourage you to reflect deeply on God's purpose for all creation?

4. Are there any events from the news this past week or any articles or books you have read that have challenged you to think more deeply about the relationship between faith and science?

5. Reflect on your current understanding of the relationship of God and the world.

6. Reflect on your knowledge and embrace of the current understandings of astronomy, evolution, and physics.

7. Look up the definition of the Anthropic Principle. Write it down. Reflect on it. Once you have grasped its meaning, think about the ways that an understanding of the Anthropic Principle can contribute to a meaningful conversation between faith and science.

8. Read and reflect on Psalm 8.

■ The Group Meeting

WELCOME those attending and, if anyone is new, ask for brief introductions. Remind the participants about the purpose of this series. Open with prayer if you choose.

READ   Psalm 8   *(2 minutes)*

Have a volunteer read it, read it together, or play Audio File 2-4 to hear Ted Peters read the first few verses. If possible, read the passage in different translations.

> O Lord, our Sovereign, how majestic is your name in all the earth! You have set your glory above the heavens.
>
> Out of the mouths of babes and infants you have founded a bulwark because of your foes, to silence the enemy and the avenger.
>
> When I look at your heavens, the work of your fingers, the moon and the stars that you have established;
>
> what are human beings that you are mindful of them, mortals that you care for them?

Yet you have made them a little lower than God, and crowned them with glory and honor.

You have given them dominion over the works of your hands; you have put all things under their feet,

all sheep and oxen, and also the beasts of the field,

the birds of the air, and the fish of the sea, whatever passes along the paths of the seas.

O Lord, our Sovereign, how majestic is your name in all the earth!

DISCUSS *(5 minutes)*

Take a few minutes to reflect on this psalm.

- Share some of the images of God that you find in it.

- Share images of the cosmos you see in it.

- How does the psalm describe the relationship between God and humans? Between God and the creatures?

- What do you notice about the psalm's literary structure?

WATCH Video 2 *(3 minutes)*

Ted Peters says Christians believe that God created one world, and that is the world that scientists are examining.

THINK AND SHARE *(10 minutes)*

Divide into groups of two. Ask each other how you experience God's revelation in the cosmos. Be prepared to share your ideas about these questions with the larger group:

- Does God reveal secrets or mysteries of the cosmos to scientists?

- Does God reveal those secrets or mysteries only to people of faith?
- How do Christians read the book of nature, and what can they learn from it?

DISCUSS (5 minutes)

Briefly talk about these questions as a whole group:

- What is the cosmos?
- How big is the cosmos?
- What does the cosmos include?
- How do you think of God acting in the cosmos and the cosmos reflecting God's work of creation?
- How big is God?

Optional Activity

LISTEN Audio File 2-1 (7 minutes)

In Ted Peters's opening interview with Peter Wallace, he discusses his interest in outer space travel and its consequences:

> Our field of astrotheology is an attempt to bring theologians and astrobiologists—that's astronomers and astrophysicists and people like that—together, to work on the religious implications of outer space and also the ethical implications of traveling to space. And also we want to get ready. Maybe the day is coming—maybe tomorrow—when space neighbors will drop in on us and we want to know do we invite them over for barbecue or not.

DISCUSS

- What is your response to his comments?

- How do you think you would respond to a space neighbor on your doorstep?

- How do you think theologians and religious people should respond?

LISTEN   Audio File 2-2   *(17 minutes)*

In his sermon, Peters illustrates vividly the meaning of cosmos and reflects on the relationship of God to the world. Here is an important passage:

> Our world today is no longer limited to Planet Earth and its measly sky. By the word *cosmos* we mean the Big Bang; we mean our sun and the solar system; perhaps 400 billion stars in the Milky Way, many of which have planets like Earth, and then perhaps another 100 billion galaxies, each with 100 billion stars, and countless more planets, stretching 11 to 13 billion light-years distant from us. Our word *cosmos* means big, unimaginably *big*. Is God still bigger? Is the God of Psalm 8 now manipulating galaxies with the divine finger?

DISCUSS   *(8 minutes)*

Consider together the ways you would answer his last two questions.

- Is God still bigger?

- Is the God of Psalm 8 now manipulating galaxies with the divine finger?

Peters mentions in his sermon that:

> . . . most astrophysicists agree that our universe began with a Big Bang 13.8 billion years ago and that it may expand for another 50 to 100 billion years before it burns out like a candle.

Continue your discussion:

- What are the similarities and differences between this view of the universe—and its beginning and end—and the ways that people of faith view the universe's creation and end?

- How does Peters describe these differences in his sermon?

- Discuss the differences between thinking of God as the God of history and thinking of God as the God of nature.

- How do such ways of thinking help us recognize the differences and similarities between the approaches of faith and science to cosmological questions?

Optional Discussion

Peters mentions the Anthropic Principle in his sermon:

According to the Anthropic Principle, the initial conditions were such that intelligent life would eventually evolve. It appears that our early universe was fine-tuned so as to prepare physics for evolving biology and prepare biology for evolving intelligence.

Astronomy professor and scientist Owen Gingerich offers a response to this idea:

I accept that the physical constants have been fine-tuned to make intelligent life in the universe possible and that this is evidence for the planning and intentions of a Creator God.

Take a few minutes to discuss these ideas.

- If the conditions of the cosmos were such that intelligent life would eventually evolve, what role does God play in this scenario?

- Is it necessary for God to be a part of this scheme?

- Do we need God to explain the creation of the world? Is this a satisfactory explanation of the creation and evolution of the world for people of faith?

Optional Activity

LISTEN   Audio File 2-3   *(8 minutes)*

In his response to Wallace's question about the Anthropic Principle, Peters provides humorous and powerful insights about the conversation between faith and science.

DISCUSS

- How does the Anthropic Principle offer people of faith a way of talking about cosmos that is compatible with science?

DISCUSS   *(5 minutes)*

Peters ends his sermon by declaring:

> Our cosmos is big. But God loves each and every creature, including you and me, directly and eternally. Our God does a lot of loving.

REFLECT

- Where do you see the wonder of God's work in your world?

- Where do you see the majesty of God "in all the earth"?

CLOSING CONVERSATION *(5 minutes)*

In some translations, Psalm 8:6 reads that God has given humans dominion over God's created order ("You have given them dominion over the works of your hands").

1. What would that mean to you?

2. To your church?

3. How do you think Christians might think about this verse?

4. According to this verse, what is humanity's role in the cosmos?

FOR NEXT SESSION *(1 minute)*

Reflect on the principles of evolution, as well as on the biblical stories of creation.

• How does each of these ways of thinking of the world satisfy you?

• Think about how these two explanations might be compatible. Does evolution have room for God? Can God's act of creation be a part of evolution?

PRAYER *(1 minute)*

O God of our creation and our redemption, you've created a cosmos of such beauty, magnificence, and mystery. We thank you for our very existence, for the privilege of living as your beloved creatures. We thank you also for the message of the gospel, for the promise of the forgiveness of sins and the resurrection into your new creation. Inspire within our souls a divine love for all that you are making. *Amen.*

Creation and Evolution

We talk about having been created with free will, the ability to choose how we interact with others. We can choose loving ways or selfish ways, each with consequences. Rarely are our motives entirely unselfish—they probably can't be this side of the grave—but if we lean in the direction of more abundant life for others, we soon discover that our own life possibilities are expanded as well.

—The Rt. Rev. Dr. Katharine Jefferts Schori

■ Background

For many Christians, the greatest challenge to a meaningful conversation about faith and science is evolution. Many people of faith have difficulty reconciling the idea that all life develops through adaptation to changing environments, that life has no purpose beyond developing strategies for surviving and passing along the traits for survival to offspring, with their belief in a Creator who guides all of life. Many Christians believe that the creation stories in Genesis 1:1–2:4a offer the most meaningful picture of the creation of the world and humankind and God's activity in it.

Charles Darwin had contemplated a career as an Anglican priest and did not see any conflict in his work as a naturalist with his faith in a creator. When he published *On the Origin of Species* in 1850, he could not have imagined the enduring debates that would swirl around his ideas. While many religious leaders of the mid- and late-nineteenth century embraced Darwin's ideas and considered them optimistic—that all of life, including humankind, continues to evolve physically and mentally—others rejected his ideas as an affront to the traditional theological ideas of human sinfulness and humanity's need for God's direction and redemption.

This conflict came to a climax in 1925 in Dayton, Tennessee, when John Scopes was prosecuted for teaching evolution in public schools, in which the subject had been forbidden. The ensuing trial pitted groups of Christians against groups that believed that the scientific theory of evolution provided the best and surest description of humanity and the world.

By the mid-1960s, the conflict arose once again, pitting Christians calling themselves Creationists against groups they called Evolutionists. The debates between these groups were often unproductive since each group focused on stereotypes of the other. These groups often stressed the incompatibility of faith and science, and they seldom found common ground for discussing faith and science.

In the late 1960s a new approach to theology called *process theology* was developed. Theologians such as John Cobb and David Ray Griffin incorporated the ideas of evolutionary biology, physics, and astrophysics into theology, exploring how science provides fresh ways of thinking about God, humankind, and the world.

By the end of the twentieth century, however, a number of scientists and theologians—many of them discussed in or participating in this series—began to embrace a dialogue that focused on the common ground on which science and religion exist. They asked how evolution might be compatible with creation: Would it be possible for people of faith to accept the tenets of evolution and think of ways that God is involved in evolution? Could scientists think of creation as a moment in the evolution of the universe and humankind? These questions fueled a rich conversation, and in this session Katharine Jefferts Schori shares her insights about the ways that people of faith can think meaningfully and creatively about creation and evolution.

■ Before the Session

As the group prepares for this session, review questions raised in the previous session. Think about the challenges you have reflecting on the conversation between faith and science. In what ways is such a conversation meaningful for you? In what ways is it difficult? Consider the following questions as you prepare for this week's session.

1. Where have you witnessed the glory of the God of creation this week?

2. This week's session focuses on creation and evolution. Reflect on your feelings about the idea of evolution. When did you first learn about it? Have your feelings and thoughts about evolution changed over the years?

3. Reflect on any sermons you have heard about creation and evolution. What ideas have they taught you about the relationship between them?

4. Reflect on the Church's teachings about creation and evolution. How do you feel about those teachings? Do they help you to think more deeply about this relationship?

5. Reflect on biblical passages that you traditionally associate with creation. What do they teach you about God, humankind, and the world?

6. Can creation and evolution be compatible?

7. Read and reflect on Mark 10:17–22.

■ The Group Meeting

WELCOME those attending. Open with prayer if you choose.

READ   Mark 10:17–22   *(2 minutes)*

Have a volunteer read, read it together, or play Audio File 3-4 to hear Katharine Jefferts Schori read it. Try, if possible, to read the passage in different translations.

> As he was setting out on a journey, a man ran up and knelt before him, and asked him, "Good Teacher, what must I do to inherit eternal life?" Jesus said to him, "Why do you call me good? No one is good but God alone. You know the commandments: 'You shall not murder; You shall not commit adultery; You shall not steal; You shall not bear false witness; You shall not defraud; Honor your father and mother.'" He said to him, "Teacher, I have kept all these since my youth." Jesus, looking at him, loved him and said, "You lack one thing; go, sell what

you own, and give the money to the poor, and you will have treasure in heaven; then come, follow me." When he heard this, he was shocked and went away grieving, for he had many possessions.

REFLECT *(5 minutes)*

Take a few moments for silent reflection. Is this a biblical text that you think of immediately when you think about the conversation between creation and evolution?

- How does this passage help us think about the conversation between creation and evolution?

- What does the passage teach about human limitations?

- What does it teach about God's role in the created order?

WATCH Video 3 *(4 minutes)*

In her video commentary Katharine Jefferts Schori says:

When traditional ways of understanding who and what God is are challenged, human beings have often rejected those new insights. It takes a significant shift in worldview for faithful people to reframe their theological understanding more broadly. Yet that reframing is one aspect of repentance, turning toward God as the center of existence, rather than ourselves and our necessarily limited understandings.

DISCUSS *(3 minutes)*

- What are your thoughts about the relationship of repentance and changing one's mind regarding new scientific insights that might affect religious understanding?

LISTEN Audio File 3-1 *(5 minutes)*

In the opening interview, Katharine Jefferts Schori comments on the ways that various advances in science changed the ways that people began to read the Bible:

> Five hundred years ago when people began to realize they could define many of the details of how things work in the world around us, people began to discount the Church's role in addressing the relationship with that which is beyond us and to assume that we could figure everything out and simply dictate it. The Bible began to be read in a very different way, rather than as a series of stories that talk about relationship. People began to read the Bible as a history book or a scientific text, purposes for which it wasn't written.

REFLECT *(5 minutes)*

Spend some time quietly reflecting on the nature of the Bible and its authority for faith and practice.

- How do we read the Bible today?
- Do we read the Bible to confirm history, or to prove scientific facts?
- Do we read it as a collection of stories that teach us various facets of truth about our lives and our life with God and the world?

Optional Discussion

- Why is it difficult for people of faith to accept or trust scientific theories?
- Why are people of faith challenged by scientific facts when they are not troubled by facts the Bible teaches?

- Why is there such a great gap between faith and reason? Can rational people also be people of faith?

- Can Christians be good scientists or doctors?

- How can Christians who are scientists or doctors reconcile their faith with science?

THINK AND SHARE   *(10 minutes)*

Break into groups of two or three and discuss the following. Jefferts Schori declares that:

> God created us with brains for a reason. We are meant to test what we meet in the world around us, to look carefully. We are meant to use our brains to sort out the way in which God is calling us to act in the world around us.

- How does Mark 10:17–22 provide an example of her statement?

- Does Jefferts Schori's declaration suggest an approach to scientific endeavors that people of faith can follow?

- If so, what are the advantages of such an approach?

- How does such an approach enable people of faith and scientists to engage more fully with one another?

Optional Discussion

Jefferts Schori comes to her position as a priest and bishop from a unique perspective. She earned a Ph.D. in oceanography and worked for several years studying cephalopods—octopuses and squids. From the interview, here is her reflection on her work as an oceanographer:

I've always been fascinated by the natural world and its richness of diverse creatures. When I was early in graduate school, I worked on things that live in the sediments in the near shore environment, and I very much wanted to work on systematics on describing species and their differences. And I looked around and discovered that there was a sizable collection of cephalopods—of squids and octopuses—already present in the laboratories where I worked, and that that was at least the launching pad for the work I wanted to do for my doctorate.... I did find a couple of new species of squid. I described the fauna that was present in the Northeastern Pacific from the northern part of Southern California up into Alaska and a long way west toward Japan. I looked at zoogeography, which is distribution in the vertical and lateral dimensions, looked at a number of fisheries' problems. We figured out how to count squid acoustically pretty effectively. Did some evolutionary theorizing and built relationships with other oceanographers across the world.

DISCUSS ways you think her work in oceanography and evolutionary biology prepared her to contribute to the conversation between faith and science.

LISTEN   Audio File 3-2   *(11 minutes)*

In her sermon, Jefferts Schori declares:

I believe three creation stories: the two in Genesis and the great creation story of cosmology and evolution. None of the three can tell us anything about what was before. All three tell us that there is a force in the universe that seems to keep creating more life or complexity. The Genesis accounts tell us that there is something, particularly about human self-centeredness, that wants to limit the abundance of other forms of life. The scientific account of creation sees chaos and stochastic processes as essential to the ongoing unfolding of what is; theologians talk about that as contingency or free will in creation.

DISCUSS *(10 minutes)*

- What are the lessons that each of these three creation stories can teach us?

- How does our embrace of these stories enable us to enhance the conversation between science and religion?

In her sermon, Jefferts Schori connects free will, sin, and extinction. Here is the passage:

> That freedom to choose is part of the nature of creation. Human beings seem to have more ability to change their environment than other creatures do, but it's something of an illusion, of which we tend to be very fond. 'I don't have to conserve water in a drought—I'll just use what I want and not worry about it.' Well, there are short-term and longer-term consequences: a higher water bill or, in some communities, having your water shut off, as well as a diminished quality or possibility of life for my neighbors—the ones I know and the ones I haven't yet met. Eventually, behavior that ignores the challenge means no one will be able to live in that place where there is little or no water—life will be less abundant. The biblical definition for that result is the consequence of sin; the biological definition is extinction.

- Discuss ways that her reading of the passage in Mark provides a new way of understanding sin.

- How does her approach connect abundant life and humanity's willful choice to destroy that life?

Optional Activity

LISTEN Audio File 3-3 *(3 minutes)*

Peter Wallace's follow-up interview with Jefferts Schori focuses on our personal lives and decisions.

DISCUSS

- Is our self-centeredness—illustrated by the young man in Mark and by the couple in the Garden of Eden—which is often described as original sin, necessary to our survival, as Jefferts Schori points out?

- How do we live into the tension between loving ourselves and loving our neighbors?

- What broader implications does loving our neighbors have on our taking care of creation?

- In her response to the question about one thing she hoped listeners would keep in mind, Jefferts Schori says we should continually consider "how our personal decisions are made—if we are aware of the impacts on others, we are already loving the world that God has created and all its inhabitants." What might happen regarding your own personal decisions if you kept those factors in mind?

CLOSING CONVERSATION *(5 minutes)*

1. Take the last minutes of this session to list images of the abundant life.

2. Then list also the images of the destruction of the abundant life.

3. Discuss how these images compare and contrast.

4. How did this session, the sermon and discussions, expand your vision of what our freedom might have to do with loving the world?

FOR NEXT SESSION *(1 minute)*

• Reflect on the idea of eternity. Think about your ideas of time and space. How do those ideas influence your understanding of your faith?

• Reflect on your knowledge of quantum physics. Find one or two definitions of quantum physics in online science encyclopedias or dictionaries. Think about the contributions of quantum physics to the conversation between faith and science.

PRAYER *(1 minute)*

Dear God, help us to see our neighbors and the world around us with new eyes. Bring our hearts and minds and souls together so we can limit our self-centeredness for the sake of the whole world. Teach us that living abundantly includes loving our neighbors as ourselves. Help us to be aware of our impact on others so that we may love the world that God has created and all its inhabitants. *Amen.*

Quantum Physics and Eternity

Isaac Newton, following Galileo's lead, described time as a river, with a steady current that flows from the future to the present and on into the past. Newton's laws of motion, which undergird all of classical physics, are dependent on this assumption. And our own daily experience of time, with our watches and atomic clocks and GPS devices, seems to fit neatly into this metaphor. But it's wrong.

—The Rt. Rev. Nicholas Knisely

■ Background

Debates over creation and evolution as adequate explanations for the beginning and continued existence of human life and the created order have been perhaps the most public face of the conversations between faith and science. However, since the sixteenth century people of faith have also wrestled with the conclusions of physics and their impact on religious faith.

Galileo (1564–1642) challenged orthodox religious views of reality by concluding through observation that the sun, not the earth, was the center of the universe. The Church had long held that the earth was the center of the universe, and since God had created the world and all in it, the Church considered the earth as the pinnacle of God's creation. Since humankind was the pinnacle of God's creation, to challenge the place of the earth in the universe also challenged the role of God in creating the world, as well as humanity's place as God's most special creation. Galileo also used his telescope to observe the wideness of the planetary system through which the Earth traveled. Such observations raised questions for people of faith about the nature of eternity and the existence of a physical place called Heaven.

In addition, if there were planets other than the earth, did that mean that God had also created them and was in control of them? Did creatures also created in God's image inhabit them? Galileo didn't ask such questions himself, but his view of the universe led other scientists to build on his ideas and pursue questions like these that would challenge people of faith and their view of God, humanity, and creation.

By the mid-seventeenth century, Isaac Newton (1642–1726) formulated laws of motion, a theory of universal gravitation, and theories of space, time, and optics that established a mechanical explanation for the ways that planets and other celestial objects in our planetary system move. Although later in life Newton devoted much of his time to writing a biblical chronology around the book of Revelation, he continued to teach that well-regulated mechanical forces operated the universe.

By the eighteenth and nineteenth centuries, people of faith found themselves confronted with scientific views that were skeptical of a God active in the world either through creative activity or providential activity (such as miracles), and that called into question many of the very principles of faith that so many Christians had held for so long (such as a God who exists in eternity). What would eternity look like if people could now observe the physical world and its laws with a telescope? If they could now observe the limits of their universe and its activities, how could people believe that the universe and its movement were limitless?

By the twentieth century, a new area of research called quantum mechanics was developed on the foundations that Newton had laid three hundred years before. Quantum physics took Newton's ideas even further to include every part of the universe, down to the very smallest particles of matter: atoms and subatomic particles. Through observation, scientists could now measure the energy of particles of matter and observe their movement through space and time. Such observations further challenged the views that a God could be active and in control of a universe whose activity was regulated by physical laws of motion.

In this session, Nicholas Knisely, bishop of the Episcopal Diocese of Rhode Island, leads us in a conversation on quantum physics and the nature of eternity as we think creatively about another aspect in the conversation between faith and science.

■ Before the Session

As the group prepares for this session, review questions raised in the previous sessions. What new insights have you gained from the speakers in the series and from your group discussions and individual reflections? What are some of the greatest challenges you have in thinking about the relationship between faith and science? What have you learned about different aspects of science? In what ways is such a conversation meaningful for you? In what ways is the conversation difficult? Reflect on the following questions as you prepare for this week's session.

1. Where have you witnessed the glory of the God of creation this week?

2. This week's session focuses on quantum physics and the nature of eternity. What do you know about quantum physics? What would you like to learn about it? How how would you describe eternity?

3. Reflect on the ways that you experience time.

4. Reflect on sermons you have heard about eternity and God's existence in eternity. What ideas have they taught you about a religious understanding of time and space?

5. Reflect on ways that various biblical passages describe time and space. How do these descriptions help you understand your own experience of time and space? In what ways are those biblical descriptions different from the ways you experience time?

6. Look up and reflect on definitions of quantum physics in encyclopedias. Bring them with you to the group for discussion and questions.

7. Read and reflect on Job 38 and Mark 10:35–45.

■ The Group Meeting

WELCOME those attending. Open with prayer if you choose.

Note: There are two Scripture passages for this session; the first, Job 38, is optional.

READ   Mark 10:35–45   *(2 minutes)*

Have a volunteer read, read it together, or listen to Bishop Knisely read it by playing Audio File 4-4. Try, if possible, to use different translations.

> James and John, the sons of Zebedee, came forward to him and said to him, "Teacher, we want you to do for us whatever we ask of you." And he said to them, "What is it you want me to do for you?" And they said to him, "Grant us to sit, one at your right hand and one at your left, in your glory." But Jesus said to them, "You do not know what you are asking. Are you able to drink the cup that I drink, or be baptized with the baptism that I am baptized with?" They replied, "We are able." Then Jesus said to them, "The cup that I drink you will drink; and with the baptism with which I am baptized, you will be baptized; but to sit at my right hand or at my left is not mine to grant, but it is for those for whom it has been prepared."
>
> When the ten heard this, they began to be angry with James and John. So Jesus called them and said to them, "You know that among the Gentiles those whom they recognize as their rulers lord it over them, and their great ones are tyrants over them. But it is not so among you; but whoever wishes to become great among you must be your servant, and whoever wishes to be first among you must be slave of all. For

the Son of Man came not to be served but to serve, and to give his life a ransom for many."

THINK AND SHARE   *(5 minutes)*

Gather into groups of two or more and discuss the images of God, humanity, and the world that this passage presents.

- What images of time and eternity does Mark 10:35–45 portray?

- List two central features of eternity and God that the reading in Mark presents.

Optional Activity

READ   Job 38

This is a very long chapter, so the group can focus on Job 38:1–7, 31–41 if time is limited. Have a volunteer read or read it together. Use different translations if possible.

Then the Lord answered Job out of the whirlwind: "Who is this that darkens counsel by words without knowledge? Gird up your loins like a man, I will question you, and you shall declare to me.

"Where were you when I laid the foundation of the earth? Tell me, if you have understanding. Who determined its measurements—surely you know! Or who stretched the line upon it? On what were its bases sunk, or who laid its cornerstone when the morning stars sang together and all the heavenly beings shouted for joy? . . .

"Can you bind the chains of the Pleiades, or loose the cords of Orion? Can you lead forth the Mazzaroth in their season, or can you guide the Bear with its children? Do you know the ordinances of the heavens? Can you establish their rule on the earth?

"Can you lift up your voice to the clouds, so that a flood of waters may cover you? Can you send forth lightnings, so that they may go and say to you, 'Here we are'? Who has put wisdom in the inward parts, or given understanding to the mind? Who has the wisdom to number the clouds? Or who can tilt the waterskins of the heavens, when the dust runs into a mass and the clods cling together?

"Can you hunt the prey for the lion, or satisfy the appetite of the young lions, when they crouch in their dens, or lie in wait in their covert? Who provides for the raven its prey, when its young ones cry to God, and wander about for lack of food?"

THINK AND SHARE   (5 minutes)

Reflect on this passage in groups of two or three, discussing the images of God, humanity, and the world that the Job passage presents.

- What are some of the lessons that Job 38 teaches about the nature of time and space and God's place in it?

- What image of God does Job 38 portray?

- List two central features of eternity and God that this passage presents.

WATCH   Video 4   (3½ minutes)

Nicholas Knisely shares insights on God, time, and the universe in the light of both science and the Bible.

THINK AND SHARE   (10 minutes)

Divide into small groups of two to four.

- Have each group list and reflect on scientific laws that govern the universe.

- Have the groups also make a list of and reflect on the divine laws they believe govern the universe.

In the larger group have each small group present its lists.

- Where do the scientific and divine laws intersect?

- Is it possible for people of faith to explain the operations of the universe in exclusively scientific terms?

- In what ways can the universe exist and operate without God?

Optional If You Read Job 38

- How does the passage in Job address this question? Does God's answer in Job address this question adequately?

Optional Activity

LISTEN   Audio File 4-1   *(5 minutes)*

In Wallace's opening interview, Knisely responds:

> I think we're moving in the latter part of the twentieth century and the beginning of the twenty-first century from an understanding of human being as individual only, to an understanding of human being as part of community. And in a sense, community becomes the dominant metaphor; the network becomes the model for how we understand what it is to be human. Somewhere in that network God exists and is completely entangled up with us. And it's that idea that we had extended beyond our own boundaries; we are connected one and another. It redefines what it is to be human, redefines what it is to experience life.

LISTEN   Audio File 4-2   *(17 minutes)*

In his sermon Knisely discusses time and eternity.

THINK AND SHARE   *(10 minutes)*

Break into groups of two to discuss your own understanding of time.

- How do you deal with time?

- How do you describe or define time?

- How do the Gospels depict Jesus defining time?

- How can we understand Jesus's view of time?

- Does such an understanding help us grasp the meaning of eternity?

Knisely raises similar questions in his sermon:

> If you look carefully in other places in the Gospels, Jesus makes a number of predictions about what is to come. And he describes things that happened in the distant past as if he were an eyewitness. While he lives a mortal life on earth, eating and sleeping and dying like any other human, he seems to also have the ability to perceive events outside of the experience of the normal flow of time. This prediction of the deaths of James and John is just one example of this ability.

Optional Discussion

Bringing your thoughts from your previous small group conversation, discuss together Knisely's questions noted above.

- How can we hope to understand Jesus's idea of time given our understandings of time?

- Do the Bible or Church teachings offer any helpful clues?

Optional Discussion on Job

In his sermon, Knisely presents an interesting reading of Job 38 in light of his own explanation of quantum physics:

> Job, I am a being that speaks from eternity, where cause and effect do not mean the same thing as what you experience. What I created out of the chaos of the beginning of your reality in a portion of the universe is ultimately beyond a finite creature's full comprehension. There is a reason and a purpose to everything I do. But it is ultimately impossible to explain to a being who cannot perceive the full reality and lives within a shadow portion of the whole.

- Take a few minutes to discuss as a group the ways that this reading improves your understanding of God, time, and eternity.

- Can people of faith ever arrive at a satisfactory explanation of time and their being in the universe?

LISTEN Audio File 4-3 *(3 minutes)*

In the interview following his sermon, Knisely distinguishes between our quest for knowledge and our need for certainty and truth:

A rabbi once told me that God hides the truth from us and expects us to use our minds, the reason that God gifted us at our birth to uncover the truth. I find it fascinating that we have this itch in us to make sense of what is probably, ultimately, un-sensible. It's the pilgrimage; it's the struggle to understand that transforms us. It's not the answer.

THINK AND SHARE *(10 minutes)*

Take a few moments to respond to his thoughts with a partner.

- Do you feel the need to make sense of the "un-sensible"?

- Do you think that having faith in the "un-sensible" provides an answer to the complexities of reality?

- Do you feel as if you need an answer to all the questions you have about life and the world around you?

- Does faith provide answers for you?

- How do Knisely's comments address the complexities of the conversation between faith and science?

Optional Discussion

Thinking about God, time, and eternity as Knisely does has moral consequences, too. Divide into smaller groups of two or three. Have each group discuss the problem of evil.

- Why do bad things happen to good people?

- Why does it sometimes seem that innocent people suffer?

- In this context discuss a recent example in which large numbers of people have been injured or died due to natural circumstances such as hurricanes, tornadoes, earthquakes, or other event.

- Share recent or personal examples of innocent people suffering injury, poor health, or death.

- Reflecting on Knisely's explanation of the relationship between quantum physics and religion, how can we answer questions such as: Where was God in this event? How could God allow this to happen? What is God's purpose for allowing this event to happen?

CLOSING CONVERSATION *(5 minutes)*

In the opening interview Knisely shares his sense of his own vocation:

> I learned to be not a scientist who happened to be a priest or a priest who happened to be a scientist, but a priest who was trained as a scientist and used that scientific training to understand God and to serve the Church.

1. Reflect together on some ways that his understanding of his vocation can help us enter the conversation between science and faith more productively and fruitfully.

2. Do you see any parallels between your own vocation, occupation, or activities and his calling?

FOR NEXT SESSION *(1 minute)*

Be thinking about these questions:

- What does "the image of God" mean to you? How does it define you? What does it tell us about human beings as a whole? Is the phrase limiting in any way?

- If humans are created in the image of God, does that mean they are also created in God's likeness? What is the difference between "likeness" and "image"?

- Can a scientific definition of humanity be reconciled with a picture of humanity made in the image of God?

- Read Genesis 1:1–2:4a, giving particular attention to Genesis 1:26–27.

PRAYER *(1 minute)*

Dear God, show us the glory, wonder, and fullness of the universe. Reveal to us the ways that you are continuing to draw out of the chaos and senselessness of our world your deeper order and purposes. Bring us healing for our pain and renewal of our hope for these moments in our lives as we seek to live more fully here and now. Thank you for showing us the beauty and purpose of the world in the life of Jesus, in nature, in Scripture, and in the Church. *Amen.*

Science and the Image of God

Insight into the intricate makeup of a human being that science provides does not discredit, diminish, or make obsolete the ancient story that we are created in the image and likeness of God. That story predates the rise of science. To be sure, it is a story that is updated and enriched by science.

—The Rev. David Wood

■ Background

What does it mean to be created in the "image and likeness of God"? What does it mean to be God-like? Does being created in the image and likeness of God make us more than human? Or better or higher than the animals and the natural world around us? As creatures made in God's image, how are we supposed to relate to nature? Are we part of nature, or are we apart from nature?

The story of creation in Genesis 1:26–27 was written down probably sometime around 500 BCE, after many Jews had returned from exile in Babylon. In 586 BCE, the Babylonians destroyed Judah and the Temple in Jerusalem; they took Jews into captivity in Babylon. Suddenly the Jews found themselves landless, leaderless, and lost in a strange land. The first lines of Psalm 137—also written around 500 BCE—declare the bitter agony and despair the Jews felt at having lost their land and their religious center: "How can I sing the Lord's song in a strange land?" Once the Persians defeated the Babylonians and Cyrus issued an edict that released the Jews from captivity, many of them returned to Jerusalem to rebuild their lives, which included rebuilding the walls of the city and the Temple.

During these years, a new class of leaders arose to mediate between God and humans—the Priestly class. As their name suggests, the priests focused on creating order and establishing liturgical reform in Jerusalem and especially in the Temple. This group collected a number of legal texts now known as the Holiness Code in Leviticus 17–26, which provided liturgical structure for the priests themselves and for worshippers of God in the Temple. They collected the lyrics of songs—some of them old songs that Israelites and Jews had sung over centuries—into a songbook called the Psalms. Psalm 8, for example, celebrates the glory and order of God's creation of the world in Genesis 1:1–2:4a.

The writers and editors of the Priestly class also focused on retelling ancient stories for a new time and a new context. What would it be like to retell the story of Creation in a new land where people had returned to reclaim the land they believed God had given them? What would it be like to retell the story of Creation to listeners who felt rejected by God, who felt that this God had taken their land from them by sending them into exile (Jeremiah

39, 52)? Why should these people worship the God who had sent them into exile in Babylon?

Genesis 1:1–2:4a retells the story of Creation from the perspective of those whose lives, land, and livelihoods had been destroyed by the Exile. The writers focused on a new creation where land is the first element created out of a chaotic absence of land. As the story proceeds, the land is repopulated and at the pinnacle of the creation story God creates human beings in God's own image. What better way for the writers to assure the dejected Jews, who felt abandoned by God, than to tell a story in which God creates humans as the very pinnacle of creation, as the highest act of creation in the story? According to the writers, God saves the "best" for last, and this story emphasizes, among other lessons, that humans are so worthy in God's sight that God creates human beings in God's image and likeness.

By the second and third centuries in the Common Era, Christian theologians tell a slightly different story; writers from Tertullian to Augustine focus not on human worthiness but on human shortcomings. Later theologians such as Martin Luther, John Calvin, and Karl Barth, among others, take up this focus on human unworthiness. Thus, in theological interpretation at least, there has been division over the ways that we can understand what it means to be created in God's image. If that image is tarnished by unworthiness, how can that image be polished so that it shines like new? Is such restoration ever possible? Can we ever again celebrate being created in God's image in the same ways that the listeners to Genesis 1:26–27 could celebrate?

Such questions become even more complicated when we approach the image of human beings from the perspective of science. As we noticed in the last session on quantum physics, Galileo and Newton, among others, established the accepted view that the earth is not the center of the universe and that mechanical laws and *not* divine purpose govern its movement. In such a view of the world, if the world that God created is no longer the center of the universe and human beings are the pinnacle of that world, then human beings are no longer worthy of being considered as the highest, most special creation of the Creator God.

In the eighteenth century, a group called the Deists tried to respond to this view of the world and God by claiming that God made the world like a watchmaker makes a watch. God, like the maker of the watch, did make all the intricate parts of the watch so that those parts could run the watch. God then wound the watch and set it in motion so that it would run on its own. Thus, even if God created the world and all in it, God no longer controls it. Where does humankind fit in such a world? Humans are simply part of the created order; their movements are dependent on the movements of all the other parts of the watch.

By the nineteenth century, evolutionary biology teaches that humans are part of the natural order, descended from other forms of animal life, and cannot be understood apart from their life in the web of all creatures. Human beings are not created in God's image but are genetic descendants of other life forms and other animal species whose very existence is passed along genetically to future members of the species in an attempt to preserve the species through time.

Into the twentieth century and beyond, science has probed the physical qualities that separate humans from other animals, while ecological thinkers have encouraged humans to see themselves as part of the larger created order. What roles should human beings play in this order? Do humans have more responsibility than other animals in shaping and preserving the natural order? If people of faith believe that humans are indeed created in the image of God, then how does this description of human beings help us understand what it means to be human and spiritual?

In this session, American Baptist pastor David Wood leads us in a conversation on the *imago dei*, the image of God, and the secret of life. Here we think creatively about another aspect in the conversation between faith and science.

■ Before the Session

As the group prepares for this session, review questions raised in the previous sessions. What still challenges you in thinking about the relationship between faith and science? Reflect on the following questions before this week's session.

1. Where have you witnessed the glory of God in creation this week?

2. What does it mean to you to be created in the image and likeness of God?

3. Reflect on the place of human beings in the world: Are humans part of nature, or do they stand apart from nature?

4. Reflect on the Church's teachings about human beings made in the image of God. What lessons about this subject do you recall from sermons, Sunday school classes, or lectures about humans being created in the image of God?

5. Are there differences between the ways Jews and Christians understand this idea? If so, what do you think those differences might be? What are the similarities between the ways that Jews and Christians understand this idea?

6. Reflect on science's image of humankind. In what ways does it differ from the image of humankind as being created in the image of God?

7. Read and reflect on Genesis 1:26–27.

■ The Group Meeting

WELCOME those attending. Open with prayer if you choose.

READ Genesis 1:26–27 *(2 minutes)*

Have a volunteer read, read it together, or listen to David Wood read it in Audio File 5-4. Try to use different translations.

> Then God said, "Let us make humankind in our image, according to our likeness; and let them have dominion over the fish of the sea, and over the birds of the air, and over the cattle, and over all the wild animals of the earth, and over every creeping thing that creeps upon the earth." So God created humankind in his image, in the image of God he created them; male and female he created them.

DISCUSS *(10 minutes)*

Read Genesis 1:1–25, the verses before this text. Take the next ten minutes to reflect on and discuss these verses.

- What portrait does the passage paint of God?

- What does it mean to be made in this God's image?

- What is the "likeness of God"?

- What is the difference between "likeness" and "image? Are they the same? Does one have priority over the other?

- What does it mean to "have dominion"?

- How would this passage have made its original hearers feel? How does it make you feel?

WATCH   Video 5   *(5 minutes)*

David Wood probes the implications of the discovery of DNA and the theological notion of the Image of God, and shares a story from writer Calvin Trillin that reveals "the secret of life."

THINK AND SHARE   *(5 minutes)*

Break into small groups. Discuss your response to the Calvin Trillin anecdote about his wife's young friend.

- How do you see the acknowledgment of being chosen as being the "secret of life"?

- More broadly, how does the image of God both connect us to and distinguish us from all other living creatures?

Optional Activity

LISTEN   Audio File 5-1   *(5 minutes)*

In the opening interview, Wood talks about Sir John Templeton's life mission of cultivating an understanding and experience of the relationship between science and theology or philosophy. Based on your experience so far in this study, how are you cultivating this understanding and experience personally?

Optional Activity

Materials: white paper and colored pencils, crayons, or markers

- Draw a picture of what the image of God looks like to you.

- Are there words or phrases in Genesis 1:1–27 that provide the contours of such an image?

- Are there other passages of Scripture that help you think about the image of God?

LISTEN   Audio File 5-2   *(14 minutes)*

Early in his sermon, Wood talks about the discovery of DNA and its significance for an understanding of ourselves as part of nature. Here is what he says:

> To put it simply, DNA is what all living organisms on earth have in common. It contains the molecular instructions for life. The implications of this discovery are still rippling out: from providing an understanding of how evolution actually works at the molecular level, to the mapping of the human genome, to producing a whole new range of possibilities for the treatment of disease.

THINK AND SHARE   *(10 minutes)*

Divide into groups of two. Have each person discuss their own family tree.

- How does one's ancestry help in understanding personality or physical well-being?

- How does an understanding of family ancestry help people see their connections to wider circles?

- How can a discussion of such ancestry give us insights into understanding what it means to be made in God's image?

Have a few participants share their responses to the whole group before resuming the conversation in different pairs.

THINK AND SHARE   *(5 minutes)*

Divide into different smaller groups to discuss the phrase "have dominion," then share responses and talk about it further with the whole group.

- How have you heard preachers and other religious leaders use this phrase in the past?

- How do you hear religious leaders or others using this phrase today?

- How do you understand it?

LISTEN Audio File 5-3 *(5 minutes)*

In his follow-up interview with Peter Wallace, David Wood quotes Francis Collins, director of the National Institutes of Health, as saying:

> DNA is the language God used to speak us and all other living things into being.

DISCUSS *(10 minutes)*

Throughout his sermon and the interview following it, Wood raises ethical questions.

- How do you feel about combining science and faith to talk about the essence of being human?

- List the ethical consequences that people of faith face as being created in the image of God.

- What kinds of activities are people of faith called to as a result of being created in the image of God?

CLOSING CONVERSATION *(5 minutes)*

Focusing on Genesis 1:26–27 and your discussions and reflections, write a prayer or a poem that expresses your understanding of being made in the image of God, either individually or as a group. If you have time, share a few of them.

FOR NEXT SESSION *(1 minute)*

Consider these questions:

- How are we genetically related to the other animals? How does this affect our view of ourselves as creatures singularly loved by God as created in God's image?

- What are the ethical implications of genetic research, and what are ways that the Bible can help us understand our calling to engage in conversation with such research?

- Read Revelation 5:11–14.

PRAYER *(1 minute)*

Dear God, thank you for creating the birds, the fish, other animals, and us as a part of your magnificent handiwork. Help us to see your image in every person we encounter every day. Teach us how to respond and to interact with each other and with all of creation as those who are bearers of the image of God. *Amen.*

The Bible and Genetics

Although there are significant exceptions, Christians have too often believed that because we are made in the image of God and have been given dominion over the earth, we stand far above the rest of the animals and can remain aloof regarding their welfare and indifferent to their suffering. But such a stance is not biblical.

—The Rev. Dr. Nancy J. Duff

■ Background

In several of the previous sessions, we have discussed the relationship between human beings and their environment. We've thought about the differences and similarities between describing the world as God's creation and as the result of an ongoing process of evolution. We've considered ways that people of faith might think of evolution and creation as partners in dialogue for understanding the work of God in our world and for thinking about the ways we discern the purpose of the created order and our roles in it. We've had the opportunity to consider the physical laws that govern our universe and the ways that our views of God and God's activity in the world coincide with or differ from physics' views of the order of the universe. We've thought about ways that even the smallest particles of matter contribute to our expansive and ever-evolving universe, and we've had the opportunity to discuss God's providential activity in the operations of our universe, as well as the ways that God might drive and sustain every aspect of our worlds. Finally, we've thought about what it means for the world and humans to be created in God's image, and about how humanity's being created in the image of God accounts for the connectedness of human life to other forms of life. We've reflected upon ways that we see God's image in our world, and we've also thought about the responsibility involved in being bearers of God's image.

In this session, we will consider more deeply how humans and animals are connected, as well as the ethical implications and responsibilities arising from those connections.

Until the middle of the eighteenth century, theologians and other thinkers depicted life in our world by using a hierarchical structure called the *great chain of being*. As in any other chain, each link is connected to the other, but the connections proceed from the top of the chain in a downward order. God resides at the pinnacle of the chain of being, for God as Creator has decreed the order of all being in the universe.

The chain of being is based roughly on the order of creation in Genesis 1:1–2:4a, although the great chain of being includes rungs on the ladder for angelic and demonic beings. God resides at the pinnacle of the chain and has decreed the order of beings that flow downward from God's being and creative activity. The angels occupy the link of the chain just below God so are the beings closest to God; they are pure spirit. Humans occupy the level just below the angels and just above the animals. The chain of being depicts humans as partaking of the spirit of the angels and the flesh of the animals below them. Thus, humans are flesh and spirit; they struggle all their lives to be as perfect as the angels, striving to be closer to God, as well as to avoid the fleshly urges of the animals below them in the chain. The chain of being depicts humans as the only creatures caught in this moral dilemma.

Below the humans are the animals. Depictions of the chain of being subdivided animals into wild animals and domestic animals, and the domestic animals are subdivided into groups of animals characterized by their demeanor: docile or useful, depending on humans' purposes for them. Since the Creation story in Genesis 2:4b–4:1 depicts the serpent as a deceitful creature that disrupts God's good creation, the serpent occupies the very bottom of the division of animals. Below the animals are plants; below plants are rock, minerals, and earth. The image of the chain of being gained popularity in medieval Christianity, but it grew less useful as a way of describing the universe as science challenged the hierarchy of being that the chain depicted.

In the Middle Ages, humans were less exalted creatures, occupying their place just below the angels and just above the animals. In the Renaissance, however, literature and art depicted humans as more capable of understanding the world around them through the faculties of reason and the senses. Although the medieval image of the chain of being does not allow for movement up or down the chain, the view of humans during the Renaissance certainly elevated humans to a position closer to God and farther from the animals.

During these last hundreds of years, what we now call "modern science" was born, challenging, as we have seen in earlier sessions, a static and hierarchical view of the universe; humans now no longer need to depend on God to reveal the wonders of the universe for them, for they could use scientific observation to discover such wonders for themselves. As the Renaissance grew into the Enlightenment, humans became even more like God, and in fact, if the eighteenth century redrew the chain of being, it might just put humans at the top of the chain and God somewhere near the bottom of the chain. Relying solely on reason, humans investigated the limitations of religious faith, embraced the freedom to make choices based on the rational examination of facts, and challenged conventional religious understandings of God's creative activity in the world, as well as conventional religious understandings of faith and revelation. During these years, animals never rose to a different level in the hierarchy because humans continued to see animals as creatures separate from themselves, and humans continued to treat animals as creatures that existed to serve humans.

By the nineteenth century, the chain of being fell out of use as a way of depicting the structure of the created order. Darwin's writings about evolution provided new insights into humans' relationships to the created order, especially to animals. He viewed animals as creatures always adapting to their environments in order to survive and to transmit their genetic structure to future generations of their species. The process of evolution is dynamic and depends on constant change within individuals and species. Humans are also part of this evolutionary scheme. As animals, humans participate in the same process of adaptation and survival as other animals. Evolutionary biology forced humans to recognize that they could no longer see themselves as higher than the animals.

By the twentieth century, evolutionary biology had taken Darwin one step further, arguing that humans and animals are connected genetically and, more strongly, that human qualities such as altruism and selfishness originated in human genes and were not qualities of behavior taught by culture or family. Such views raised enormous questions for people of faith, including the origins of religion. If the human disposition to being religious is genetic, then the gene will eventually pass away when humans no longer need to develop religion in order to adapt and survive. Such views raise larger questions such as: How should humans treat each other? Is there any difference between being religious and being moral? How should humans treat animals?

In this session, Princeton theologian and ethicist Nancy Duff leads us in a conversation on the Bible and genetics, especially humans' relationship with animals, as we think creatively about another aspect in the conversation between faith and science.

■ Before the Session

As the group prepares, review questions raised in previous sessions. What challenges and questions do you still have in thinking about the relationship between faith and science? Reflect on the following questions in advance of the group meeting.

1. Where have you witnessed the glory of God in creation this week?

2. Do you have pets at home? How do you treat them? Do you think of them as members of your family?

3. Have you ever lived or worked on a farm? Be prepared to talk about your experience with others in the session.

4. Reflect on the nature of farming in the twenty-first century from what you know about it. How are animals treated on farms?

5. Reflect on the advantages and disadvantages of genetic research on humans and animals. Be prepared to discuss your thoughts in the group meeting.

6. Reflect on the many biblical passages that feature and focus on animals. What biblical images of animals are most meaningful to you?

7. Read and reflect on Revelation 5:11–14.

▪ The Group Meeting

WELCOME those attending. Open with prayer if you choose.

READ   Revelation 5:11–14   *(2 minutes)*

Have a volunteer read, read it together, or listen to Nancy Duff read it using Audio File 6-4. Use different translations if possible.

> Then I looked, and I heard the voice of many angels surrounding the throne and the living creatures and the elders; they numbered myriads of myriads and thousands of thousands, singing with full voice, "Worthy is the Lamb that was slaughtered to receive power and wealth and wisdom and might and honor and glory and blessing!" Then I heard every creature in heaven and on earth and under the earth and in the sea, and all that is in them, singing, "To the one seated on the throne and to the Lamb be blessing and honor and glory and might forever and ever!" And the four living creatures said, "Amen!" And the elders fell down and worshiped.

REFLECT *(10 minutes)*

Invite individuals to journal or reflect quietly on the following:

- What leads up to this passage in Revelation 5?

- What else do you know about the Revelation of John?

- Does this particular passage surprise you? What is your emotional response when you hear this passage?

- What lessons does this passage teach us about worship?

- How does this passage depict the glory and unity of creation?

- Why worship a wounded lamb and not a lion?

WATCH Video 6 *(4½ minutes)*

In the video Duff says the first theological question she ever had was whether animals go to heaven.

THINK AND SHARE *(5 minutes)*

Break into pairs and discuss:

- What do you think about this question?

- How do you respond to her comments about genetic experiments in animals?

- How does the attitude of the writer of the Revelation toward animals influence your response?

DISCUSS

Take a few minutes to share ideas about how you or your group could be more intentional about seeking more information about scientific efforts today, and how to evaluate and respond to them.

LISTEN   Audio File 6-2   (13 minutes)

In her sermon, Nancy Duff refers to findings from an article on genetics:

> Science affirms this common origin by saying we all sprang from the same DNA. Although evolution took us in different directions: humans share 98.5 percent of our genetic makeup with the chimpanzee, 79 percent of our genetic makeup is shared with the mouse, and 36 percent with the common fruit fly.

DISCUSS   *(5 minutes)*

- If science confirms our common lineage with animals, what does this say about human origins and humanity's place in the created order?

- How does this scientific information match up with the picture of human and animal origins in the creation story in Genesis 1?

- Does this information from genetics give you a reason to think any differently about your relationship to animals?

THINK AND SHARE   *(10 minutes)*

Nancy Duff talks about the promise and limitations of being human in her sermon:

> Though we have dominion over the earth (Genesis 1:26), the power we have over animals is meant to reflect God's care for them. Not one word in the Bible gives us leave to take advantage of that power by being cruel or indifferent to the lives animals lead or to the suffering and deaths they endure sometimes at our hands. No such cruelty or indifference is found in God.

In small groups, consider these questions:

- How do we participate in the suffering and deaths of animals?

- In what ways have we been cruel to animals?

- Where have you witnessed cruelty to animals, and how have you reacted?

- Think about agribusiness, or large factory farms: how are animals treated at such facilities?

- What do you think a person's cruel and indifferent treatment of an animal says about that person?

Optional Discussion

- If genetic testing and research in animals inflicts unwarranted suffering on animals, can we justify genetic testing and research on animals?

- Should we engage in genetic testing and research on animals solely for the benefit of humans? What does this tell us about our understanding of Genesis 1:26–27?

THINK AND SHARE *(10 minutes)*

In her sermon, Duff reflects on the thoughts of twentieth-century theologian Karl Barth:

> Barth warned against "our astonishing indifference and thoughtlessness" toward animals, insisting that we keep in mind that killing an animal is not the same as harvesting a plant, and that we cannot justify cruel treatment of animals by looking to nature where animals seem cruel to one another, because unlike any other animal, we alone were created in the image of God and given dominion over the earth. We do not look to nature but to

God to define our relationship with the animal world—and God has given us responsibility for them. Finally, Barth reminds us that animals belong *not* to us but to God—a claim that should make Christians question the practice of filing for patents on genetically modified animals as if they were no different than machines that belong to their inventors.

In pairs or triads, discuss one or more of these ideas:

- Some now argue that harvesting a plant has much the same moral force as killing an animal. Think about the reasons we kill animals or harvest plants; is there a biblical mandate for the correct, moral way to kill animals or harvest plants?

- Focus on the last point about animals belonging not to us but to God. How does this help us understand the ways we should act toward animals?

Optional Activity

Read Revelation 5:11–14 (which is a hymn). Divide into groups of two or three and compose your own poem or hymn in which the animals in your own homes, on surrounding farms, in the woods or meadows or lakes, rivers, or in the oceans that surround us all sing God's praises. As you do, think about how we might sing with them.

CLOSING CONVERSATION

LISTEN   Audio File 6-3   *(4 minutes)*

In this closing interview, Nancy Duff expresses her hopes that Christians can come to a different understanding of their relationship to all creation, especially animals:

I'd like Christians not to feel insulted when science—evolutionary science—says that we are closely related to some animals, and rather rejoice in how God has put us in such close relationship to the primates, and science affirms that we share a great deal of DNA with them. But I'd also like people to consider that even the strangest animals that live at the bottom of the deepest sea, which we will never actually encounter, are also part of God's creation. So that everything we do that has to do with the environment has to do with the other creatures that God has made and called good. So in a very positive way I would like us to be encouraged to lead our lives so that we do less harm to God's creation and, most specifically, the animals.

DISCUSS   (5 minutes)

1. Describe how this session has made your position on our relationship with animals more complicated.

2. Make a list of all the ways you can treat animals ethically as part of taking care of God's good and full creation.

3. Determine next steps for implementation.

FOR NEXT SESSION   (1 minute)

Think about these questions:

- For you, what is the promise of eternal life?

- Is death a natural part of life?

- Given advances in medical technology, should we take steps to prolong life and avoid death? What does it mean to die a good death?

- Read Psalm 90.

PRAYER *(1 minute)*

We thank you, God, for creating all that dwells within the world—and for calling it good. Give us the wisdom to preserve what you have created. We thank you for giving us dominion over the earth. Help us to wield the power that is ours with grace and compassion. We thank you for sending your Son to set creation free from its bondage to decay. Teach us to join all living creatures in praising your holy name, singing: "To you be blessing and honor and glory and might for ever and ever." In Christ's name we pray, *Amen.*

SESSION

7

Life and Death

When we gain the deep knowledge that we are limited in days and incomplete in ourselves, this can draw us ever closer to the God who is immortal and who brings our life to completion.

—The Rev. Dr. Thomas G. Long

■ Background

Contemporary medical technology has progressed so far that it has developed various techniques to prolong human life beyond the time when such life might otherwise have expired.

For thousands of years, humans have struggled with their finite limits: the frailness that accompanies aging, physical debilitations of disease, the ravages inflicted upon the body by hunger brought on by famine, and death itself. Humans desired to live forever, and ancient stories often depict humans striving to become like the immortal gods, not only living eternally but also being in control of all life.

When humans faced death, they surrounded themselves with their families and communities who retold stories, recited formulas, and practiced rituals in hopes of carrying the dying person's soul over into the next world where it would be guaranteed immortality. The desire to live forever dwells deep in the human psyche, so human beings have warmly and enthusiastically greeted developments in modern medicine as a promise of something closer to immortality.

Yet, even with such advances in medical technology, we fear death. We are frightened to let go of life, to leave behind our loved ones and the warm and loving communities of which we are a part. We are terrified of the unknown. We are so involved with our bodies that we are fearful of what will happen to them after we die. We know our days are numbered, but we put off counting the days we are given. Ironically, even though we fear the knowledge that we have a certain number of days to live, we can embrace this knowledge of our limited time and live life to its fullest.

Confronting questions of life and death brings the conversation between faith and science into our lives in direct and potent ways. If we are part of the web of nature, being born and dying like other animals, shouldn't we simply accept our deaths as part of our lives? Why should we fear death? How does our faith help us accept death? Does the hope of life in God after death give us confidence in a future that helps us cope with life and death in this world? Does a focus on an eternal life distract us from living this life fully?

In this session, Tom Long, the Bandy professor of preaching emeritus at Candler School of Theology at Emory University, leads us in a conversation about death and eternal life as we think creatively about another aspect in the conversation between faith and science.

■ Before the Session

As the group prepares, review questions raised in previous sessions. What challenges and questions do you still have regarding the relationship between faith and science? Reflect on the following questions as you prepare for this week's session.

1. Where have you witnessed the glory of God in creation this week?

2. When is last time you attended a funeral? How did the pastor or religious leader describe the person's life and death?

3. In what ways do you measure the quality of your life, or the lives of others close to you?

4. Reflect on the many passages that focus on life and death, and life after death. Do they have any images in common? If so, what are some of those images?

5. Reflect on Tom Long's statement: "In the Gospel I think death is a defining characteristic of being human. Being mortal is what it means to be human, and so to refuse to acknowledge our mortality is a big way of getting things wrong." Be prepared to discuss your thoughts with the group.

6. How do you "number your days"? Is this phrase hopeful or frightening?

7. Read and reflect on Psalm 90.

■ The Group Meeting

WELCOME those attending. Open with prayer if you choose.

READ Psalm 90:1–4, 10, 12   *(2 minutes)*

Have a volunteer read, read it together, or listen to Tom Long read it with Audio File 7-4. Try, if possible, to read the passage in different translations.

> Lord, you have been our dwelling place in all generations. Before the mountains were brought forth, or ever you had formed the earth and the world, from everlasting to everlasting, you are God.
>
> You turn us back to dust, and say, "Turn back, you mortals." For a thousand years in your sight are like yesterday when it is past, or like a watch in the night. . . .
>
> The days of our life are seventy years, or perhaps eighty, if we are strong; even then their span is only toil and trouble; they are soon gone, and we fly away. . . . So teach us to count our days that we may gain a wise heart.

DISCUSS   *(5 minutes)*

- How do you feel when you hear this passage?
- What does it mean to "number our days"?
- How do we "number our days" in the modern world?

WATCH   Video 7   (5½ minutes)

Referring to Psalm 90, Tom Long says:

> Notice that when the psalmist prays to God to teach us to number our days, the yearning is not for more and more days, but to have the kind of life that enables us to be formed well as human beings, to have a wise heart, to have a life that matters.

DISCUSS   *(3 minutes)*

- Why do you think humans tend to desire "more and more days" rather than focusing on how to live wisely a life that matters?

THINK AND SHARE *(10 minutes)*

Divide into smaller groups or pairs. Discuss what it means to die a good death. List the definitions or descriptions your group has discussed so you can share them with the larger group.

- How do you define a "good death"?
- How does science help make it possible to die a good death?
- In what ways do biblical teachings describe a good death?
- Do you ever think about your own death?
- Are you afraid of dying? If so, why? If not, why not?
- Are there any specific biblical passages that comfort you when you think about your own death?

DISCUSS *(10 minutes)*

Invite everyone to return to the larger group and share insights from their conversations. Then consider these questions together:

- How is Jesus's death a model for our own dying and death?
- Consider Jesus's approach to his own death in the various places in the Gospels that describe it.
- Can we die like Jesus died?

Optional Think and Share

As individuals, try to come up with five biblical passages that deal with death.

- In each passage, what happens to the body when it dies?
- What happens to the soul?

Regroup and compare lists with other members of the group; discuss the different ways that each passage describes death.

DISCUSS   *(5 minutes)*

- Where does the soul reside?

- How do biblical writers describe the relationship between the soul and the body?

- Do you think about the relationship between your body and your soul? If so, how?

- What happens to your soul when you die?

bay. And in the Gospel I think death is a defining characteristic of being human. Being mortal is what it means to be human, and so to refuse to acknowledge our mortality is a big way of getting things wrong. We try to escape into flights of fancy that we can be youthful forever and live forever, not face up to our mortality.

DISCUSS

As a group, discuss these questions:

- What forces in our culture reinforce this kind of thinking?

- Why are we so frightened about death that we don't think about it?

- Turn to the person next to you and tell them what frightens you most about death. Ask that person what frightens them most about death.

LISTEN   Audio File 7-2   (16 minutes)

Tom Long's sermon on death and dying encourages us to "number our days."

DISCUSS   *(10 minutes)*

In the whole group, consider these questions:

- How do *you* "number your days"? *Have* you numbered your days? That is, do you count the days before some special event, anticipating the fellowship and fun you expect to have at this event?

- Do you nervously count the days and minutes before a medical procedure, or before a big meeting at work, or a test at school?

- What pleasure and profit does numbering your days bring you?

- Have you numbered your days in a more literal way, thinking that the Bible says we'll live seventy or eighty years, so that you might not live beyond that?

Optional Discussion

- What are some ways that genetic engineering promises to defeat death?

- Is the promise of a longer life through medical technology more relevant at the beginning of life than at the end? That is, would we wish to take heroic measures to prolong the life of an infant with cystic fibrosis, sickle cell anemia, or Down syndrome? What about an older person: Would we wish to take heroic measures to prolong the life of a patient with Alzheimer's or Parkinson's disease, or a person who has suffered a stroke or has terminal cancer?

In his sermon, Tom Long compares the medical view of life and its longevity with the biblical view of the length of life:

The psalmist reminds us that when we look at life through the eyes of faith, the goal is not simply the quantity of life, but the quality of life—the depth and breadth and height of life, not just its length. What makes life good is not just longevity, not just living more and more days, but becoming a certain kind of person—a person whose heart is wise before God.

And it is right at this point that our faith must raise a provocative challenge to modern medicine. While people of faith join with all others in giving thanks for the many ways that medicine gives us strength and health and freedom from unrelenting pain, what must be challenged is the false idea that the only way to seek a good life is the never-ending quest for more of it, for more and more days, for longer and longer lives. And lying just beneath the surface of this medical quest for unending life is the false promise, the science fiction dream, even the idolatrous claim, that science and medicine will one day give us immortality, that someday medicine will genetically engineer death out of the human equation—the dream that human beings on biological grounds can live forever and that living forever would be a good thing.

DISCUSS these remarks as a group.

- How do people of faith today balance the tension between their desire to maintain a good *quantity* of life with their desire to preserve a good *quality* of life?

- Does this understanding help assuage your fears about death, if you know you have experienced a "life well lived"?

CLOSING CONVERSATION

LISTEN   Audio File 7-3   *(3 minutes)*

In his closing comments, Tom Long encourages us to find balance in the tension between the approaches of faith and science to life and death:

> God is the God of Life. So every bit of life is precious and we should seize life and drink it down to the bottom and enjoy it. On the other hand we are not God. We are not immortal, and to acknowledge the limitations of being human is something that presses us toward that which is beyond us.

DISCUSS   *(5 minutes)*

1. What response do you have to Long's words?

2. How do you try to find balance when you're thinking about life and death?

3. How do you affirm that God is the God of life?

BEFORE NEXT SESSION   *(1 minute)*

- Think about some ways that people of faith and scientists can continue to have a fruitful conversation about their differences and their similarities.

- Consider the ways your thinking about your faith has been challenged during this series.

- How might churches and people of faith more meaningfully engage in matters of science?

- Read Acts 19:1–7.

PRAYER   *(1 minute)*

Dear God, give us the wisdom to see that our life resides in your life. Give us the strength not to be afraid of aging or death no matter where we find ourselves in life, whether we're young or old, or in full strength or failing body. Help us to remember that you are love and that your grace is infinite. Teach us to number our days so that when we come to the end we can be confident in the assurance that the risen Christ will be there to receive us and to say to us, "You are home now. You have a place at the table. There is plenty to go around." *Amen.*

Continuing the Conversation in the Churches

There's so much more to learn, and it is an expression of grace that we have the capacity to still learn and the opportunity to be taught by others when we don't fully comprehend. Continuing education is a gift as we keep inquiring and listening and being curious and open to new ideas and fresh experiences.

—The Rev. Dr. Luke Powery

■ Background

If we are open to the world around us, we see new parts of it every day. We might notice the color of the winter sky as it changes every day of the week. We might see the swirl of water in the ocean as the waves recede in patterns that we've never noticed before. We see for the first time the homeless man or woman at the corner and glimpse the sorrow in their eyes. We meet old friends and discover that each is aging in surprising ways. We see acts of hate or of love and disregard them or react in anger or joy to them. If we are open, we are always learning about our world, others, and ourselves. Learning continues through our lives, and nature or books or art or music or science or others continue to teach us.

For many, learning occurs in institutions set apart to educate them. They may attend sixteen years of school and decide their education is complete; they never want to hear another lecture or speech, do another science experiment, or read another book again. Our society often acts as if learning is confined to those years, urging high school or college graduates to launch right into the workforce and thus separating education (schooling) from work.

As you have learned over these sessions, this artificial separation of schooling and work could not be further from the truth. We're always learning—or, better yet, we always have the opportunity to learn if we're willing to be taught, willing to be made uncomfortable with new knowledge, and willing to be challenged by new ideas and information, testing it, questioning it, and putting it into conversation with all we have already learned. Certainly these sessions have challenged us to consider our understandings of various aspects of science, as well as to think about the ways that faith and science can engage in a productive conversation.

In this concluding session, Luke Powery, dean of Duke University Chapel, leads us in a conversation about ways that we might continue the conversation between faith and science in our churches.

■ Before the Session

As the group prepares for the final session of this Faith and Science series, review questions raised in the previous sessions. What challenges and questions do you still have regarding the relationship between faith and science? How has this series changed your thinking about the relationship between science and faith? How does your church participate in conversations about faith and science in your community? What are some ways that your church can more actively participate in such conversations? How can your church actively lead such conversations? Reflect on the following questions as you prepare for this week's session.

1. Where have you witnessed the glory of God in creation this week?

2. What areas of science are most interesting to you, and in what areas of science would you like to engage in more conversation with scientists or medical professionals? What are some ways you can engage in such conversations?

3. Where do you see connections between science and faith in your daily life?

4. Make a list of the scientists and theologians with whom you would like to engage about some of the topics discussed in the series. Look for books or articles by them in your local bookstore or library.

5. Plan to continue the conversation by starting a discussion group on faith and science one morning, afternoon, or evening a month.

6. If possible, invite local speakers—perhaps from nearby colleges and seminaries—to address your church on some of the topics we've covered in the series, or those we haven't, such as neuroscience and faith (Where is the soul? Does the soul exist?) or medical ethics.

7. Read and reflect on Acts 19: 1–7.

■ The Group Meeting

WELCOME those attending. Open with prayer if you choose.

READ   Acts 19:1–7   *(2 minutes)*

Have a volunteer read, read it together, or listen to Luke Powery read the passage with Audio File 8-4. Try to use different translations.

> While Apollos was in Corinth, Paul passed through the interior regions and came to Ephesus, where he found some disciples. He said to them, "Did you receive the Holy Spirit when you became believers?" They replied, "No, we have not even heard that there is a Holy Spirit." Then he said, "Into what then were you baptized?" They answered, "Into John's baptism." Paul said, "John baptized with the baptism of repentance, telling the people to believe in the one who was to come after him, that is, in Jesus." On hearing this, they were baptized in the name of the Lord Jesus. When Paul had laid his hands on them, the Holy Spirit came upon them, and they spoke in tongues and prophesied—altogether there were about twelve of them.

DISCUSS *(5 minutes)*

Reflect together on this passage.

- Read and think about the verses that come just before and after these verses.

- How do you feel when you hear this passage?

- What are the main obstacles to learning? How can we overcome them?

- What is Paul's point about the meaning of discipleship in this passage?

WATCH Video 8 *(4 minutes)*

Luke Powery encourages people of faith to continue their inquiry into science and keep learning.

DISCUSS *(5 minutes)*

- How do *you* best learn? Simply by listening to a speaker present new ideas? Or by taking notes while you're listening to a speaker or while reading? Or some other way?

- What is your biggest challenge in learning and absorbing new ideas?

- Do you like to be challenged by new ideas and information?

REFLECT *(3 minutes)*

Reflect individually on the following:

- List three ways that your views of faith and science have been challenged during this series.

- In what areas would you like to learn more?

DISCUSS *(10 minutes)*

God reveals Godself through nature, the Church, the Bible, and Jesus. For many Christian thinkers, God's revelation though nature is only partial and requires God's revelation through Jesus for it to be a complete revelation of God's purposes. Faith is our response to God's revelation. As a group list ways that God reveals Godself through nature, and discuss the ways that your faith grows through these moments of revelation.

- What new facets of God are revealed to you in such moments?

- How do these moments increase your understanding of God and nurture your faith?

- Would your faith be diminished without such moments?

LISTEN Audio File 8-2 *(13 minutes)*

In his sermon, Luke Powery challenges us:

> We know that we don't know but can have an open heart and mind, a teachable spirit, to learn something new every day. We have so much more to learn and God has so much more to teach us. But do you possess a humble, holy curiosity? Are you teachable?

THINK AND SHARE *(5 minutes)*

Work in groups of two or three to answer Powery's question.

- What does it take for you to be "teachable"?
- Reflect on the ways that Paul's disciples declared themselves open to his teaching.

REFLECT *(5 minutes)*

In his sermon, Powery reflects on humans' ability to know and not to know:

> The blessing, the gift of the Holy Spirit in this story, was both unintelligibility and comprehensibility. Some things in life you just can't explain because you can't exhaust an inexhaustible God. It is a freeing gift not to know everything, and we will always be at a place of understanding and not fully understanding. That's because we're human and not God.

- Does Powery's acknowledgement of our inability to know everything comfort you?
- Does it challenge you? Does it give you a feeling of freedom?

LISTEN   Audio File 8-3   *(5 minutes)*

In Peter Wallace's closing interview following the sermon, Luke Powery reflects on how challenges to our faith can empower us:

> I think that's a great thing—to be challenged and not always comforted. You know, there's that old saying that sometimes a preacher may pray before a sermon, asking God to comfort the afflicted and afflict the comfortable. And I think change comes through being challenged, and that's why it's significant—to be changed and transformed, becoming more and more transformed into the likeness of Christ.

DISCUSS

Think about a time recently when you have been knocked out of your comfort zone of faith by a challenge to it.

- How did you respond?

- Did you welcome the challenge, or resist it? Why?

- How did you deal with the challenge as a person of faith?

CLOSING ACTIVITY   *(10 minutes)*

In the closing interview Luke Powery talks about the power of mentors to teach us when we're yearning to learn. He points out that in Acts 19:1–7 Paul's disciples accepted him as their mentor, even though Apollos, who was away in Corinth, had been their teacher. Paul taught them new ideas about which they had not heard.

Here are Powery's words:

> The disciples had Paul as an example. They had a mentor. They had a teacher, and the learning

happened in community. I think if we can help people in our churches—maybe they are in our churches already—from different fields, scientists, doctors, if we can help them come to know one another and to have conversations about their disciplines and their work as a way of informing one's own faith, I think we have to create spaces for mutual learning. And if they're not in our churches, we go outside of our own congregations and find where they are and define places where we can have these pockets of learning, which for me are pockets of hope as well.

Conclude your study with the following prompts for creating ongoing reflection, study, and action:

1. Who are the mentors in your church, in your community, in other nearby churches, who can lead conversations about their disciplines—particularly about matters of science?

2. How can you create "spaces for mutual learning" in your church? In your community?

3. How do you plan to continue your education in the realm of science and faith?

PRAYER   *(1 minute)*

Dear God, thank you for the gifts of discernment and wisdom. Help us to use those gifts as we seek to learn more about God, the world, others, and ourselves. Help us to be open to those teachers who challenge us to think beyond the borders of what we already know. Bless us with your Spirit to open our hearts and minds to the beauty, order, intelligence, and truth of our world. Move us to embrace conversation with others about our world and our lives in it, and sustain us in those conversations. Thank you, God, for these opportunities to explore and to learn. *Amen.*

For Further Reading

Barbour, Ian. *Religion and Science: Historical and Contemporary Issues* (San Francisco: HarperSanFrancisco, 1997). This is a revised and expanded edition of an earlier book titled *Religion in an Age of Science* (HarperSanFrancisco, 1990). Even though Barbour's book is just over twenty years old, it still offers an excellent overview of and introduction to the major issues in the conversation between religion and science.

Bass, Diana Butler. *Grounded: Finding God in the World.* (San Francisco: HarperOne, 2015.)

Berry, Wendell. *The Unsettling of America: Culture and Agriculture.* Reprint edition (Berkeley, CA: Counterpoint Press, 2015).

Brown Taylor, Barbara. *An Altar in the World: A Geography of Faith.* (San Francisco: HarperOne, 2009).

Dillard, Annie. *Pilgrim at Tinker Creek: A Mystical Excursion into the Natural World* (New York: Bantam Books, 1975).

Dixon, Thomas. *Science and Religion: A Very Short Introduction* (New York: Oxford, 2008).

Dyson, Freeman. *Disturbing the Universe* (New York: Harper, 1979).

Gawande, Atul. *Being Mortal: Medicine and What Matters in the End* (New York: Metropolitan Books, 2014).

Gingerich, Owen. *God's Planet* (Cambridge, MA: Harvard University Press, 2014).

Hoezee, Scott. *Proclaim the Wonder: Engaging Science on Sunday* (Grand Rapids, MI: Baker, 2003).

Johnson, Elizabeth. *Ask the Beasts: Darwin and the God of Love* (Bloomsbury: Continuum, 2015).

Knisely, W. Nicholas. *Lent Is Not Rocket Science.* (New York: Morehouse Publishing, 2013).

Long, Thomas G. *Accompany Them with Singing: The Christian Funeral* (Louisville: Westminster John Knox, 2013).

McFague, Sallie. *Supernatural Christians: How We Should Love Nature* (Minneapolis: Fortress Press, 1997).

Orbiter Magazine website. http://www.orbitermag.com

Peters, Ted. *God in Cosmic History: Where Science & History Meet Religion* (Winona, MN: Anselm Academic, 2017).

Pope Francis. *Laudato Si: On Care for Our Common Home* (Maryknoll, NY: Orbis Books, 2016).

Powery, Luke. *Spirit Speech: Lament and Celebration in Preaching* (Nashville: Abingdon Press, 2009).

Powery, Luke. *Dem Dry Bones: Preaching, Death, and Hope* (Minneapolis: Fortress, 2012).

Sacks, Jonathan. *The Great Partnership: Science, Religion, and the Search for Meaning* (New York: Schocken Books, 2014).

Sacks, Oliver. *The River of Consciousness* (New York: Knopf, 2017).

Wallace, Paul. *Stars Beneath Us: Finding God in the Evolving Cosmos.* (Minneapolis: Fortress Press, 2015).

Web of creation website, http://www.webofcreation.org/

Wilson, E.O. *The Origins of Creativity* (New York: Liveright, 2017).

Wilson, E.O. *On Human Nature* (Cambridge, MA: Harvard, 1978).

Meet the Speakers

The Rev. Dr. Nancy J. Duff is the Stephen Colwell Associate Professor of Christian Ethics at Princeton Theological Seminary in Princeton, New Jersey. She earned her MDiv from Union Presbyterian Seminary in Virginia and a PhD from Union Theological Seminary in New York. An ordained minister in the Presbyterian Church (U.S.A.), she focuses her research on the theological foundations of Christian ethics. Writing from the Reformed tradition and informed by both Pauline apocalyptic and feminist concerns, she explores how theological claims identify the Church's responsibility in the world. She teaches courses in the theology and ethics of Dietrich Bonhoeffer, the theology and ethics of James Cone, issues in biomedical ethics, human sexuality, the doctrine of vocation, and the ethics of the Ten Commandments.

■

The Rev. Scott E. Hoezee is director of the Center for Excellence in Preaching at Calvin Theological Seminary. Ordained in the Christian Reformed Church in North America, he served as the pastor of Second Christian Reformed Church in Fremont, Michigan, from 1990–1993 and Minister of Preaching and Administration at Calvin CRC in Grand Rapids, Michigan, from 1993–2005. In 2005, he became the first director of the Center for Excellence in Preaching. He has also been a member of the Pastor-Theologian Program sponsored by the Center of Theological Inquiry in Princeton, NJ, where he was pastor-in-residence in the fall of 2000. From 2001–2011 Hoezee served on the editorial board of *Perspectives: A Journal of Reformed Thought* and was co-editor of that journal from 2005–2011. He is the author of several books including *The Riddle of Grace*, *Flourishing in the Land*, *Remember Creation*, *Speaking as One: A Look at the Ecumenical Creeds*, *Speaking of Comfort: A Look at the Heidelberg Catechism*, and *Proclaim the Wonder: Preaching Science on Sunday*.

■

The Rt. Rev. Dr. Katharine Jefferts Schori was the twenty-sixth Presiding Bishop of the Episcopal Church, and now serves as Assisting Bishop in the Diocese of San Diego. Bishop Jefferts Schori's career as an oceanographer preceded her studies for the priesthood, to which she was ordained in 1994. She holds a BS in biology from Stanford University, an MS and PhD in oceanography from Oregon State University, an MDiv from Church Divinity School of the Pacific, and several honorary doctoral degrees. She served as assistant rector at the Church of the Good Samaritan, Corvallis, Oregon, where she had special responsibility for pastoring the Hispanic community (she speaks Spanish fluently). She remains an active, instrument-rated pilot—a skill she applied when traveling between the congregations of the Diocese of Nevada, where she was elected bishop in 2000. At the time of her election as bishop of Nevada, she was a priest, university lecturer, and hospice chaplain in Oregon. She is the author of several books.

■

The Rt. Rev. W. Nicholas Knisely was elected to be the thirteenth Bishop of Rhode Island in 2012. As a graduate student at the University of Delaware, Knisely decided to leave behind his studies of Physics and Astronomy and was sent to Yale/Berkeley Divinity School to study for the priesthood. He was ordained to the priesthood in 1992. Knisely served as a priest in Delaware, Western and Eastern Pennsylvania, and as dean of the Cathedral in Phoenix, Arizona. He has been active in a number of ministries with particular focus in the areas of homelessness, communications, college and youth, finance, and ecumenical relations. He taught physics and astronomy for nearly seven years at Lehigh University while he was serving in Bethlehem, Pennsylvania. He was the first chair of the General Convention of the Episcopal Church in America Standing Commission on Communications and Technology and was part of the Moravian-Episcopal Dialog that drew up the full communion agreement between the two denominations. He has written extensively on the relationship between science and faith, including *Entitled States: Science and Faith* and *Lent Is Not Rocket Science.*

■

The Rev. Dr. Thomas G. Long is Bandy Professor of Preaching Emeritus at Candler School of Theology, Emory University. His research interests are contemporary homiletical theory, biblical hermeneutics, and preaching. His book, *What Shall We Say? Evil, Suffering, and the Crisis of Faith*, explores questions of God and human suffering, and was named "2011 Book of the Year" by the Academy of Parish Clergy. Long's 1989 book *The Witness of Preaching*—now in its second edition—is one of the most widely used texts on preaching, appearing on class reading lists in seminaries across the country and world. In 2010, *Preaching* magazine named *The Witness of Preaching* one of the twenty-five most influential books in preaching for the last twenty-five years. Long's *Preaching from Memory to Hope* was named as one of the "top ten books for parish ministry published in 2009" by the Academy of Parish Clergy. The author of more than twenty books, Long is a frequent contributor to *The Christian Century* and the *Journal for Preachers*, and a popular presenter at preaching conferences worldwide. He holds an MDiv from Erskine Theological Seminary and a PhD from Princeton Theological Seminary, and is an ordained minister in the Presbyterian Church (USA).

■

The Rev. Dr. Ted Peters is an ordained pastor in the Evangelical Lutheran Church in America. He is Research Professor Emeritus in Systematic Theology and Ethics at Pacific Lutheran Theological Seminary, the Center for Theology and the Natural Sciences, and the Graduate Theological Union in Berkeley, California. He offers a theological analysis of culture, analyzing especially the role of science in culture. He co-edits the journal *Theology and Science*. He has also served as science and religion editor for religion in *Geschichte und Gegenwart, Volumes IV–VIII*, and for the *Encyclopedia of Religion*, second edition, 2005. During the first decade of this century, Peters worked with his colleague in evolutionary biology and virology, Martinez Hewlett, publishing three books on the culture war over evolution—the war between atheists, creationists, intelligent design advocates, and theistic evolutionists.

■

The Rev. Dr. Luke A. Powery is the dean of Duke Chapel and an associate professor of the practice of homiletics at Duke Divinity School. Prior to his appointment at Duke, he served as the Perry and Georgia Engle Assistant Professor of Homiletics at Princeton Theological Seminary. He received his BA in music with a concentration in vocal performance from Stanford University, his MDiv from Princeton Theological Seminary, and his ThD from Emmanuel College, University of Toronto. His teaching and research interests are located at the intersection of preaching, worship, pneumatology, performance studies, and culture, particularly expressions of the African diaspora. He has written two books, *Spirit Speech: Lament and Celebration in Preaching* and *Dem Dry Bones: Preaching, Death, and Hope.* Nurtured in the Holiness-Pentecostal tradition, Powery was ordained by the Progressive National Baptist Convention, and has served in an ecumenical capacity in churches throughout Switzerland, Canada, and the United States. He served as a member of the executive lectionary team for *The African American Lectionary.* In 2008, the African American Pulpit named him as one of "20 to Watch," an honor given to twenty outstanding black ministers under the age of forty who are helping to shape the future direction of the Church.

■

The Rev. David J. Wood is senior minister of Glencoe Union Church in Glencoe, Illinois. An ordained American Baptist pastor, he has served various congregations for nearly thirty years, including churches in Maine; Paris, France; Kentucky; and Connecticut. He studied theology and ministry at Gordon Conwell Theological Seminary and Yale Divinity School. Wood also serves as a consultant to the John Templeton Foundation—assisting in the development of programs that stimulate a more intelligent and interesting engagement between science and faith in the life of congregations in North American and around the world.

■

The Rev. Peter M. Wallace, editor, is the executive producer and host of the national ecumenical "Day1" radio and internet ministry (Day1.org) and president of the Alliance for Christian Media, based in Atlanta, Georgia. The weekly Day1 radio program, the voice of the mainline churches, is distributed to more than two hundred radio affiliates across America and overseas, and as a podcast on a variety of platforms. Wallace is the author of ten books, including *Getting to Know Jesus (Again): Meditations for Lent*; *The Passionate Jesus: What We Can Learn from Jesus about Love, Fear, Grief, Joy, and Living Authentically*; *Connected: You and God in the Psalms*; **and** *Living Loved: Knowing Jesus as the Lover of Your Soul.* He earned a bachelor's degree in journalism/advertising from Marshall University and a Master of Theology degree from Dallas Theological Seminary, Dallas, Texas. He took Anglican Studies courses at Candler School of Theology at Emory University. He has been a confirmed member of the Episcopal Church since 1991, was ordained as an Episcopal priest in 2014, and serves in the Diocese of Atlanta.